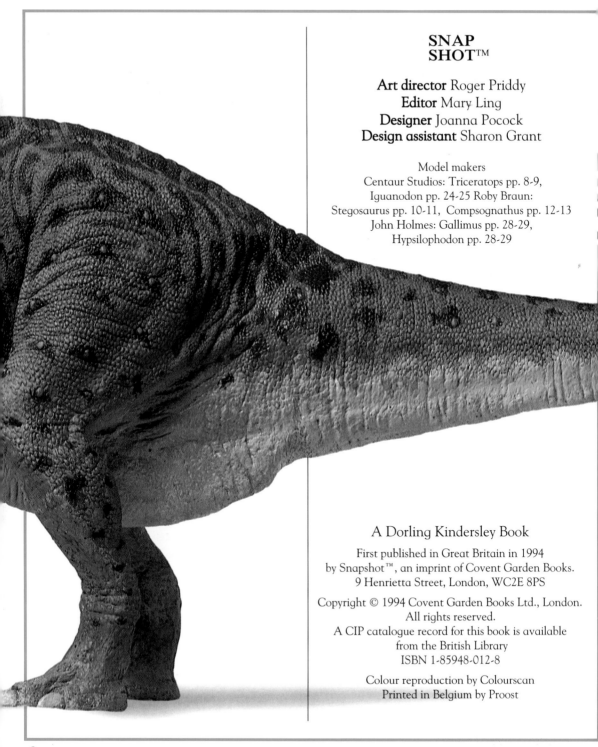

# SNAP SHOT™

**Art director** Roger Priddy
**Editor** Mary Ling
**Designer** Joanna Pocock
**Design assistant** Sharon Grant

Model makers
Centaur Studios: Triceratops pp. 8-9,
Iguanodon pp. 24-25 Roby Braun:
Stegosaurus pp. 10-11, Compsognathus pp. 12-13
John Holmes: Gallimus pp. 28-29,
Hypsilophodon pp. 28-29

## A Dorling Kindersley Book

First published in Great Britain in 1994
by Snapshot™, an imprint of Covent Garden Books.
9 Henrietta Street, London, WC2E 8PS

A CIP catalogue record for this book is available
from the British Library
ISBN 1-85948-012-8

Colour reproduction by Colourscan
**Printed in Belgium** by Proost

# INCREDIBLE
# DINOSAURS

Written by
Christopher Maynard

# Contents

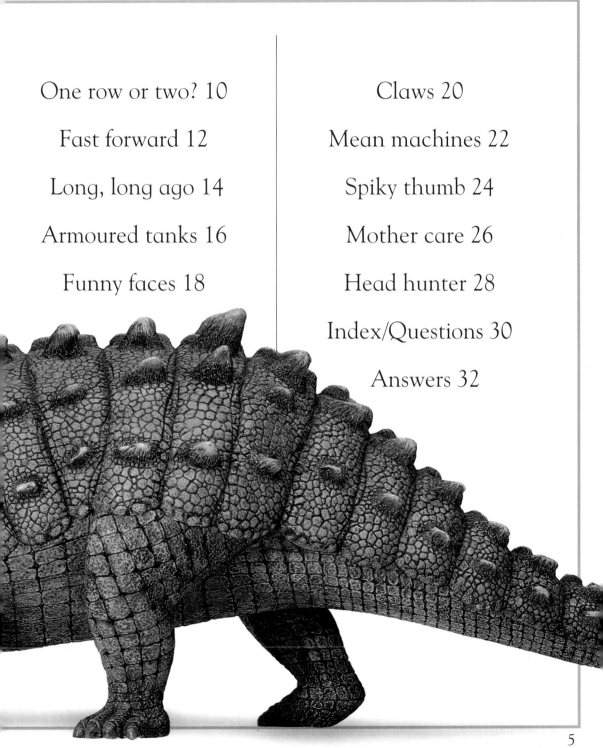

# Big tooth

*Tyrannosaurus* was king of the meat-eaters. It killed its prey with its wicked scooping bite. It even attacked the biggest game, including giants like *Triceratops*.

Serrated tooth

**Snap!** When a tooth broke off, a new one soon grew in its place.

Teeth as big as kitchen knives

# Bigger and heavier than an elephant

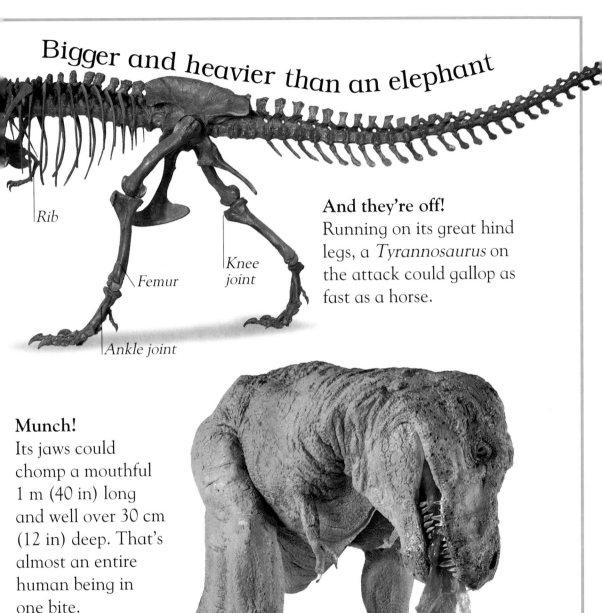

Rib

Femur

Knee
joint

Ankle joint

**And they're off!**
Running on its great hind
legs, a *Tyrannosaurus* on
the attack could gallop as
fast as a horse.

**Munch!**
Its jaws could
chomp a mouthful
1 m (40 in) long
and well over 30 cm
(12 in) deep. That's
almost an entire
human being in
one bite.

# A head with three horns

Think of an elephant. Then add a hooked beak, huge horns and a frill of thick bone. What you end up with is a *Triceratops!*

**Big frill**
When a *Triceratops* lowered its head to charge, the frill made its face look twice as big and dangerous.

It was as much a rhino as a dino

Frill

Brow hor

Nose horn

**Heavy head**
It would take all your muscles to lift a *Triceratops* skull.

**Long horn**
The twin horns above its eyebrows might grow as long as an adult human being.

*Wavy edge of frill*

## What food did it eat?

**Toothless beak**
*Triceratops* used its great hooked parrot's beak to nip through tough plants. Behind it were rows of teeth that sliced up the plants still more.

# One row or two?

When the fossils of *Stegosaurus* were first found, dinosaur hunters thought the huge bony plates lay flat on its back. They called it "roofed lizard".

**Big nosher**
*Stegosaurus* was a plant eater. As it weighed almost two tonnes, it spent most of the day browsing on plants to satisfy its huge hunger.

**Tilt!**
With its shorter front legs and its small head near the ground, it could reach low growing plants.

or radiators? A giant with a brain as big as a walnut!

**Wobble**
The plates were attached to the skin, not to the skeleton.

**Central cooling**
The plates controlled body temperature. When it was hot they gave off heat. When it got cold, they soaked up warmth.

Dorsal plate

Femur

Ulna

Chevron

# Fast forward

*Compsognathus* was a tiny dinosaur built for speed. It darted about chasing after small lizards and insects. With its thin legs and bird-like feet it was a very fast runner.

**Stal**
It had dozens of tiny razor sharp teeth

**Tiny dino**
You could lift *Compsognathus* in one hand. It was no bigger than a chicken.

**Eye spy**
Like a bird, it had big eyes to help find and track down small, fast-moving prey.

## meat-eating chicken that bites

Jaw muscle

Forelimb

Thigh

Claw

Hallux (first toe)

**Fine fossil**
Its tiny bones were beautifully preserved in a bed of fine mud. One skeleton even had the remains of a last lizard meal in its stomach.

# Long, long ago

Nose to tail, the *Barosaurus* stretched 27 m (88 ft). That's almost as long as a blue whale or three buses!

All neck and tail, with a very tubby tummy

**Giants**

*Barosaurus* and its relatives were the biggest animals ever to walk on land. Next to them, a grown-up elephant looks like a baby.

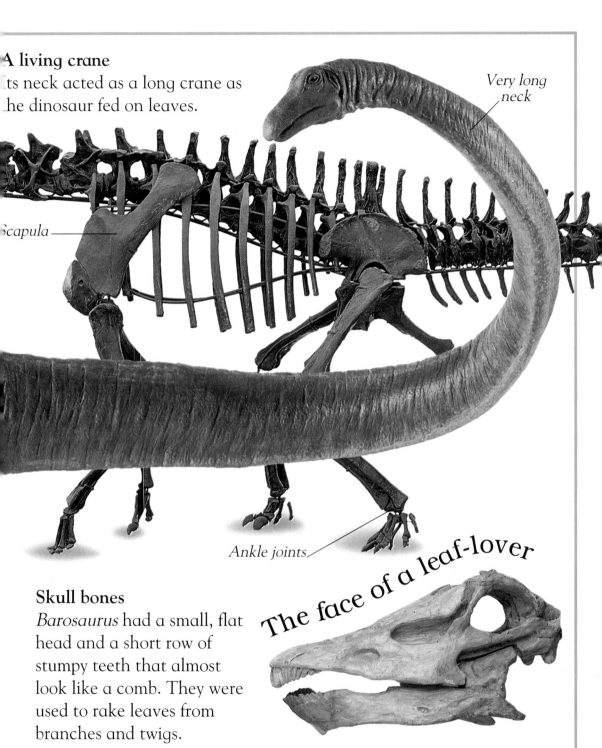

## A living crane
Its neck acted as a long crane as
the dinosaur fed on leaves.

*Very long
neck*

Scapula

Ankle joints

The face of a leaf-lover

## Skull bones
*Barosaurus* had a small, flat
head and a short row of
stumpy teeth that almost
look like a comb. They were
used to rake leaves from
branches and twigs.

# Armoured tanks

The most heavily armoured dinosaurs of all were the *Ankylosaurs.* These giants were covered with thick leathery skin, plates of bone and horny spikes.

## Join the club

At the end of the heavy tail were two thick lumps of bone. They joined together to turn the end of its tail into a great club.

## Low blow

Its heavy tail could swing hard from side to side and cripple the legs of any hunter that came too close.

So well armoured they never had to run away

Tail club

Shoulder
spike

Armoured tail

Hind foot

**Slow and low**
Really big *Ankylosaurs* might
weigh three tonnes or more with all that heavy
armour. But they were only as tall as
your front door!

**Bone helmet**
The eyes peered out
from under a shield
of bone.

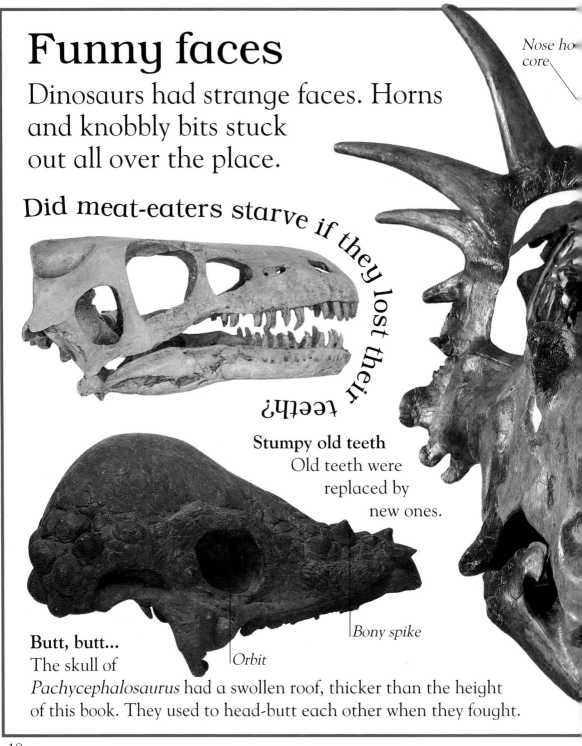

# Funny faces

Dinosaurs had strange faces. Horns
and knobbly bits stuck
out all over the place.

Did meat-eaters starve if they lost their teeth?

Nose horn core

**Stumpy old teeth**
Old teeth were
replaced by
new ones.

*Bony spike*

*Orbit*

**Butt, butt...**
The skull of
*Pachycephalosaurus* had a swollen roof, thicker than the height
of this book. They used to head-butt each other when they fought.

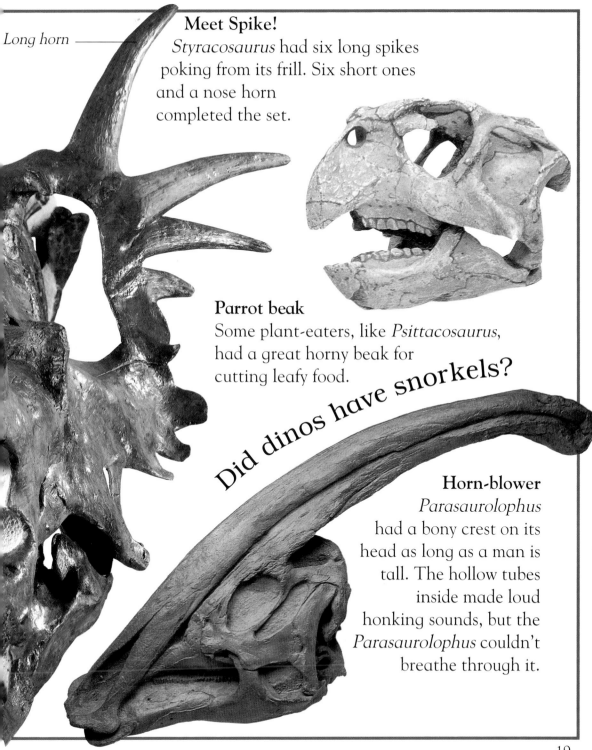

Long horn

### Meet Spike!
*Styracosaurus* had six long spikes poking from its frill. Six short ones and a nose horn completed the set.

### Parrot beak
Some plant-eaters, like *Psittacosaurus*, had a great horny beak for cutting leafy food.

## Did dinos have snorkels?

### Horn-blower
*Parasaurolophus* had a bony crest on its head as long as a man is tall. The hollow tubes inside made loud honking sounds, but the *Parasaurolophus* couldn't breathe through it.

# Claws

In 1982 a giant dinosaur claw was found in a quarry. Its outer curve alone would stretch right across this open book. *Baryonyx* was a big meat-eater.

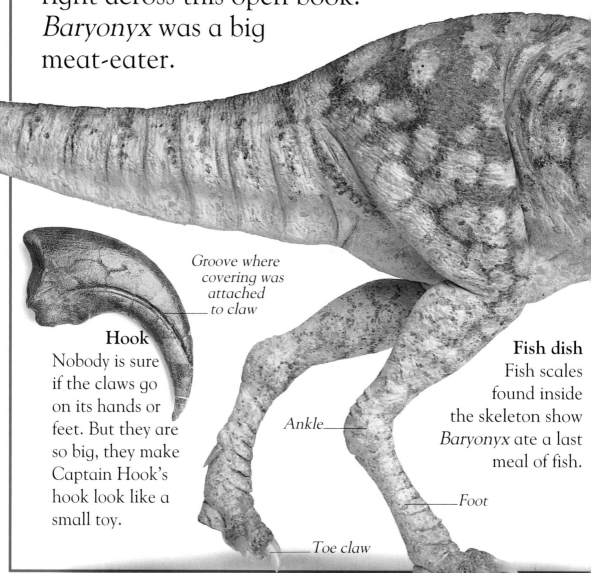

Groove where covering was attached to claw

**Hook**
Nobody is sure if the claws go on its hands or feet. But they are so big, they make Captain Hook's hook look like a small toy.

Ankle

Foot

Toe claw

**Fish dish**
Fish scales found inside the skeleton show *Baryonyx* ate a last meal of fish.

### Long jaw
*Baryonyx* had long, flat jaws, which remind people of a crocodile. It is quite likely it ate fish regularly.

**Why did this dinosaur love to go fishing?**

### Toothy grin
With 32 sharp teeth to grip with on each side of its jaw, no slippery fish would have had a chance to escape.

### Gone fishing
Like a bear, it waded in the shallows and hooked out its catch with its great claws.

**Is this the smile of a crocodile?**

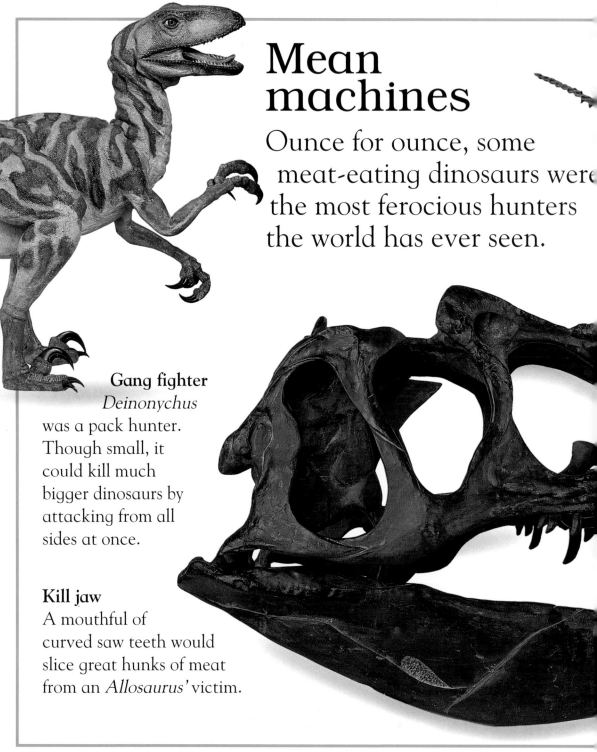

# Mean machines

Ounce for ounce, some meat-eating dinosaurs were the most ferocious hunters the world has ever seen.

**Gang fighter**
*Deinonychus* was a pack hunter. Though small, it could kill much bigger dinosaurs by attacking from all sides at once.

**Kill jaw**
A mouthful of curved saw teeth would slice great hunks of meat from an *Allosaurus'* victim.

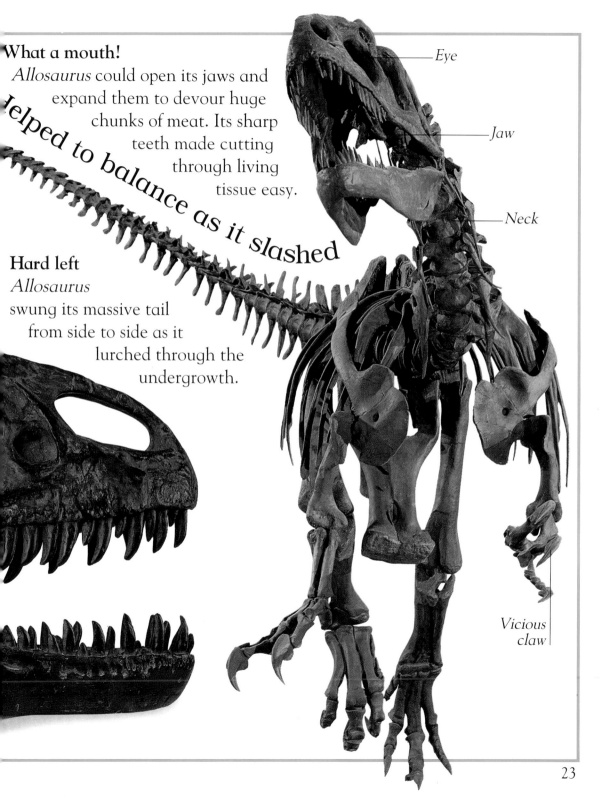

## What a mouth!

*Allosaurus* could open its jaws and expand them to devour huge chunks of meat. Its sharp teeth made cutting through living tissue easy.

—Helped to balance as it slashed

## Hard left

*Allosaurus* swung its massive tail from side to side as it lurched through the undergrowth.

Eye

Jaw

Neck

Vicious claw

23

# Spiky thumb

Plant-eaters all had different ways to protect themselves from attack. In the case of *Iguanodon*, a big, spiky claw on its thumbs was used as a weapon.

A tail prop for sitting up

Flexible fifth finger

**On all fours**
*Iguanodon* walked on all fours with its tail held straight behind. It only rose up on its hind legs to feed, or to defend itself with its spiked front claw.

## Big enough
*Iguanodon* grew 9 m (30 ft) from nose to tail, and weighed about four tonnes.

## Nip and chew
It had no front teeth, but used its beak to nip off leaves and twigs. The back of its mouth was full of wide, flat chewing teeth.

*Beak*

## Thousands of bones
*Iguanodon* is one of the best known dinosaurs of all. Dozens of skeletons have been found over the years.

*Mandible*

## Big tummy
It needed a huge stomach and intestines to digest all the food it had to eat in order to stay alive.

*Foot*

# Mother care

All dinosaurs laid eggs. *Maiasaura* took care of her young in a nest. Here, she guarded and fed them until they could fend for themselves.

*Sometimes several females laid their eggs in the same nest*

*The biggest dinosaur eggs were 30 cm (12 in) long, but most were a lot smaller*

### Earth nest

Eggs were laid in a mound of earth, then covered with soil. They stayed warm until they cracked and the babies crawled out.

Bigger than birds' eggs

# Head hunter
Can you name these
dinosaurs?

1

2

3

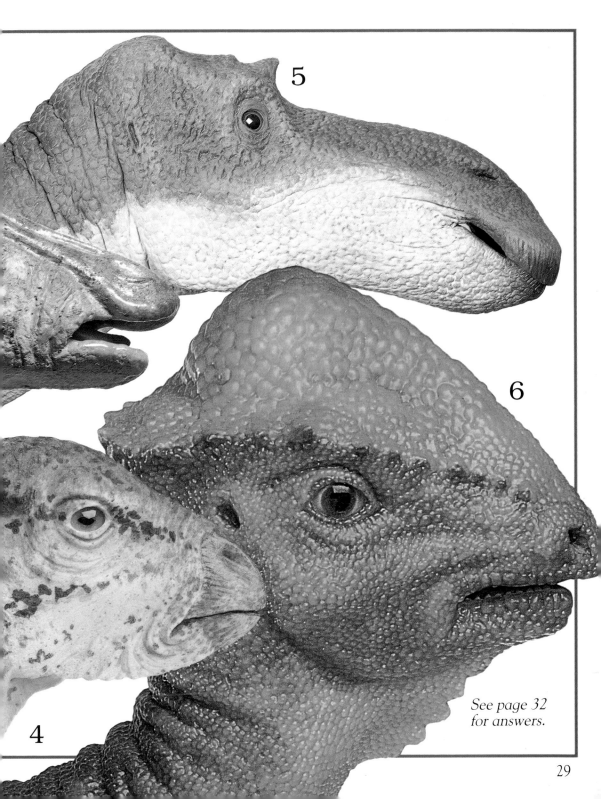

5

6

4

*See page 32 for answers.*

# Index

## Five fiendish questions

1) How many fingers did *Tyrannosaurus* have?

2) What dinosaur had plates, but never ate from them?

3) Which dinosaur could blow its own trumpet?

4) How did the fishing dinosaur catch a meal?

5) What made *Pachycephalosaurus* sometimes have a headache?

*Answers on page 32*

# Answers

From page 28-29:

1. *Gallimimus*      4. *Hypsilophodon*
2. *Troodon*         5. *Iguanodon*
3. *Corythosaurus*   6. *Stegoceras*

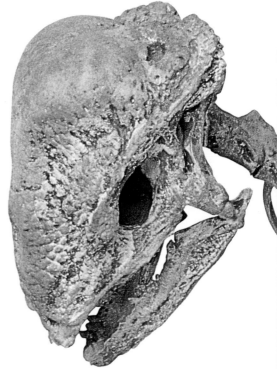

From page 30:

1. Two
2. *Stegosaurus*
3. *Parasaurolophus*
4. With its big hooked claw
5. A head-butting fight with another
   *Pachycephalosaurus*